东 龙
特色田园乡村
Donglong Characteristic Rural Area

王建国　朱渊　罗文博　著

东南大学出版社
南京

内容简介

近年来，在国家持续实施"乡村振兴战略"的大背景下，我国对"三农"问题的关注和乡村建设日益升温。随着中央一系列政策和地方实践的推进，乡村建设正走向在地化、特色化和可持续化道路。

本书中的东龙村乡村建设是"江苏省特色田园乡村建设"行动的组成部分。本书详细记述了南京江宁东龙村2017—2020年针对村域公共空间和重点建筑的改造更新设计与建设历程，在上位规划的语境下着重论述并呈现了东龙村建设实践的缘起、过程、构思设计和实施成果，通过对乡村历史文化遗存差异化的保护更新延续集体记忆，同时整合扩充公共服务设施，优化提升乡村人居环境，探索了中国特色的在地性乡村振兴的可行之路。

本书可供乡村建设相关从业者、建筑师、规划师、乡村问题研究者，以及社会公众阅读参考。

图书在版编目（CIP）数据

东龙：特色田园乡村 / 王建国，朱渊，罗文博著
. -- 南京：东南大学出版社，2024.3
ISBN 978-7-5766-1178-6

Ⅰ.①东… Ⅱ.①王… ②朱… ③罗… Ⅲ.①农村 - 社会主义建设 - 研究 - 中国 Ⅳ.① F320.3

中国国家版本馆 CIP 数据核字（2023）第 252506 号

东龙：特色田园乡村
Donglong : Tese Tianyuan Xiangcun

著　　者：王建国　朱　渊　罗文博
责任编辑：戴　丽
责任校对：张万莹
封面设计：罗文博
责任印刷：周荣虎
出版发行：东南大学出版社
社　　址：南京市四牌楼2号（邮编：210096　电话：025-83793330）
邮　　编：210096
网　　址：http://www.seupress.com
出 版 人：白云飞
印　　刷：上海雅昌艺术印刷有限公司
开　　本：889 mm×1194 mm　1/20　印张：6　字数：150千字
版 印 次：2024年3月第1版　2024年3月第1次印刷
书　　号：ISBN 978-7-5766-1178-6
定　　价：68.00元
经　　销：全国各地新华书店
发行热线：025-83790519　83791830

* 版权所有，侵权必究
* 本社图书若有印装质量问题，请直接与营销部联系。电话：025-83791830

东 龙

前言　FOREWORD

乡村，一直以来承载了诸多文化和空间意象，作为一种接近自然生态和乡土中国文化的空间载体，它与高度人工化、商业化和标准化的城市形成鲜明对比。人们常说故土难离，谈及乡村也总包含着寻根、乡愁、在地性、田园栖居等精神与场所隐喻。世界上大大小小的乡村分布广袤、数量巨大，它们孕育于不同的文化地理区域，虽常常默默无言掩盖于全球化滥觞中，却又始终涵养着最具多样性和差异性文化的人类乡土社群聚落。

中国自古"以农立国"。中国社会对"乡土"独具情怀，华夏文明的孕育和发展植根于农耕定居和周而复始的农业生产活动和民俗民风。这些农耕生产生活建构了众多依托特定气候条件、水土资源和文化生活习惯的高度组织化的乡土社会结构，并形成了中国丰富多彩的乡村地域风貌。随着近半个世纪快速的工业化和城市化进程，传统乡村的社会组织形式、有机生长状态以及地方建造技艺等都经历了深刻变革，区位资源差异和经济发展状况的落差更进一步加剧了城乡二元对立，乡村建筑的丰富性和多元化特征正面临越来越大的冲击。

2017年，习近平总书记在党的十九大报告中提出乡村振兴战略，并强调农业农村农民问题是关系国计民生的根本性问题。2018年，中共中央、国务院印发的《乡村振兴战略规划（2018—2022年）》做出具体谋划，明确提出从不同村庄的发展现状、区位和资源出发，分类推进乡村发展，并首次确定了集聚提升类、特色保护类、城郊融合类、搬迁撤并类等四类村庄的差异化发展定位。

东龙村位于江苏南京东南近郊，距主城约1小时车程，具有城乡联动发展的区位基础。同时，东龙村所在的江宁区青龙社区水土条件优越，农业基础较好，随着近年来农村电商兴起和田园旅游升温，以一系列作物培育和种植体验园为主的现代农业示范区已初具规模。2017年，东龙村入选江苏"特色田园乡村"试点项目，开始了主要针对农房更新利用、活动组织引导、田园景观一体化等方面的新发展探索和建设示范。与周边部分大量农民易业或搬迁的乡村不同，东龙村较好的农业和人口资源使其成为社区未来规划的重点保留村庄，因此如何在原有基础上通过产业升级、环境优化和空间改造，推动乡村生产、生活和生态的全面集聚提升成为本次乡村建设工作的重要命题。

我们团队有幸应邀参加了东龙村的建筑改造更新工作，在前期华诚博远工程技术集团有限公司规划设计团队的村庄建设规划基础上，进一步仔细调研了乡村的自然和人文条件。针对乡村公共设施缺乏、休闲文旅体验不足和电商服务空间需求逐年扩大等情况，我们团队同规划和自然资源局、青龙社区、产业经营和村民代表和前期规划团队等进行了多次商讨，以乡村既有闲置土地的高效利用、历史遗存的创造性保护和集体记忆的有机延续为主要原则，选定位于南侧村口的"电商街—油坊地块"和北侧中部的"油坊地块"两个重要空间节点进行改造设计和更新建设工作。经过两年多的时间，团队先后完成了围绕新青龙广场的村民中心—油坊博物馆建筑群、电商产业示范街、东龙生态餐厅及其周边的景观设计提升。目前改造更新工作已完成，村庄公共空间和服务设施容量大为提升，室内装饰和展陈布置于2020年下半年先后完成，陆续向当地村民和游客开放使用。同年，青龙社区被正式命名为江苏省级特色田园乡村。

东龙村的建筑改造更新基于对乡村自然本底和形态结构的充分尊重。东龙村的整体形态总体呈现为"田林环绕，星水伴居，悠然见山"的南北带状结构特征，设计希望新置入建筑延续这样的场地肌理，因此在重要视觉界面尽量采用小体量分散式布局，严格控制建筑尺度，采用折叠坡屋面的组合方式降低较大体量建筑对周边乡村肌理的冲击，同时通过连廊、挑檐、坡道和不同标高的景观平台系统将其串联成使用高效、空间宜人的公共建筑群。从设计到建设的过程，团队经过多次材料选用的推敲，选择当地常见的砖石、竹木构造配合轻质的钢、铝型材体系实现在地性特征和空间经济性能的平衡，并在重点节点的做法上进行了现场1:1的试做和检验。

在青龙广场、油坊博物馆广场和生态餐厅庭院等空间的塑造中，场地原有的青龙雕塑、旧厂房和沼气罐等工业设施历史遗存经过了仔细的评估，根据其质量状况和功能空间需求采用形态修复、结构置换、要素切割异地重构等差异化的保护与改造模式，与新建筑共同组合到建筑群空间环境的整体营造中，重塑场地肌理的同时延续当地村庄居民的集体记忆。

从方案构思、设计到最后落成，我们在这个过程中也体会颇多。团队在本次实践中面对的是一个从规划、产业、建筑到景观、室内、展陈的一体化设计施工项目，虽然并不负责所有的设计工作，但一定要对整个周期有全面的研究才能在不同尺度上实现对乡村历史、文化生活和地方特色的表达。同时，乡村建筑实践往往面对着较为多元的使用群体和功能需求，特别是在类似东龙村这样原住民比例较高的乡村，一定要仔细考虑外来游客和本地居民的差异化诉求，减少设计者单向的"审美价值输出"，与村集体多沟通形成良好互助的"乡建共同体"，一定程度上能弥补市场导向和标准化建造带来的与乡村真实生活的割裂。实际上我们观察到在这几组建筑落成后，不少居民以此为参考根据自身需求对自宅或门店进行了多样化的翻修尝试，可见本次乡建工作发挥了良好的示范引领作用。

东龙村建筑改造更新的竣工和运营得到了广泛的关注，收到了不少的好评。乡村产业服务业得以更充分的拓展，村民在广场举行各类特色活动，大量党建工作依托乡村会堂有序开展。但我们也清醒地知道，东龙村的乡建工作在材料耐候研究、工程进度把控、施工精度等方面仍有不少值得完善和提升的地方，期待在今后的乡村实践中吸取经验、减少遗憾。

最后，必须在此感谢在东龙村特色田园乡村项目策划、规划设计和建造过程中做出重要贡献的江宁区委区政府、南京市规划和自然资源局江宁分局、青龙社区、华诚博远工程技术集团有限公司等。

王建国

2023年6月

The countryside has always carried a lot of cultural and spatial imagery, and as a spatial carrier close to the natural ecology and Chinese vernacular culture, it stands in stark contrast to the highly artificial, commercialized, and standardized urban environment. People often say that it is difficult to leave one's homeland, and talking about the countryside always includes spiritual and spatial metaphors such as root seeking, homesickness, locality, and pastoral dwelling. There are so many rural settlements widespread throughout the world, bred in different cultural regions. They are often silently concealed in the flood of globalization but have always nourished the most multifarious and differentiated human vernacular cultural communities.

Since ancient times, China has been "a country of agriculture". Chinese society has a unique feeling for "native soil". The gestation and development of Chinese civilization are rooted in farming settlements and repeated agricultural production activities and folk customs. Farming production and life have constructed many highly organized rural social structures relying on specific climatic conditions, water and soil resources, and cultural habits, and formed the rich and colorful rural landscapes and architectural styles in China. With the rapid industrialization and urbanization of the last half century, the social organization, organic growth, and local construction techniques of the traditional rural areas have undergone profound changes, and the disparity in resources and economic development between different regions has further exacerbated the urban-rural dichotomy. The richness and diversity of rural architecture are facing increasing impact.

In 2017, President Xi Jinping put forward the "strategy of rural vitalization" in the 19th CPC National Congress, and emphasized that the issues relating to agriculture, rural areas and rural people are fundamental to China as they directly concern our country's stability and our people's wellbeing. In 2018, The National Rural Vitalization Strategic Plan (2018-2022) issued by the CCCP and the State Council made specific plans, clearly proposing to promote rural development in a categorized manner based on the characteristics, resources, and location of different villages, and determined the differentiated development positioning for four types of villages, including the clustering and upgrading category, the characteristic protection category, the suburban integration category, and the relocation and removal category.

Donglong Village is located in the southeastern suburb of Nanjing, Jiangsu Province, about one hour's drive from the main urban area, and has the location basis for urban-rural linkage development. Meanwhile, Qinglong Community in Jiangning District, where Donglong Village is located, has superior soil and water conditions with a good agricultural foundation. With the rise of rural e-commerce and pastoral tourism in recent years, a modern agricultural demonstration zone with a series of crop cultivation and planting experience gardens has begun to take shape. In 2017, Donglong Village was selected as one of the pilot projects in Jiangsu Province for the construction of "Characteristic Rural Areas", starting a new development exploration and construction demonstration mainly focusing on the building renovation, activity organization and guidance, and the integration of pastoral landscape. Different from some surrounding villages where a large number of farmers have changed their jobs or relocated, Donglong Village's better agricultural and population resources make it one of the key villages to be preserved in the future planning of Qinglong Community. Therefore, how to promote the overall clustering and upgrading of rural production, life, and ecology through industrial upgrading, environmental optimization and spatial renovation on the original basis has become an important proposition for this rural construction work.

We are honored to be invited to participate in the building renovation of Donglong Village. Based on the rural development and construction planning of Huachengboyuan Engineering Technology Group Co., Ltd., we further carefully investigated the natural and cultural conditions of this village. Because of the lack of rural public facilities, insufficient tourism experience, and the increasing demand for e-commerce service space year by year, we conducted many discussions with Nanjing Municipal Bureau of Planning and Natural Resources, Qinglong Community, some industry operators, village representatives, and the preliminary planning teams. With the main principles of efficient use of existing unused land in the village, creative conservation of historical relics, and organic continuation of rural collective memory, two important sites located next to an old oil mill at the entrance of the village and a biogas station in the middle of this village were selected for architectural renovation and renewal design. After more than two years, we have completed the building group of the village center and oil mill museum around the new Qinglong square, the e-commerce demonstration street, the Donglong ecological restaurant, and the landscape enhancement around them. At present, the renovation and renewal work has been completed, and the overall public space and service facilities capacity of the village has been greatly enhanced. The interior decoration and exhibition layout have been completed successively in the second half of 2020, and are gradually opened to local residents and tourists. In the same year, Qinglong Community was officially named as one of "Characteristic Rural Areas" in Jiangsu Province.

The architectural renovation and renewal design of Donglong Village is based on full respect for the rural ecological substrate and morphological structure. First of all, distributed in a north-south direction along the road, Donglong Village presents the characteristics of being "surrounded by fields and forests, accompanied with water ponds and mountains". Our design hopes that the newly placed buildings will continue this kind of site texture, so a small volume and decentralized layout is adopted at important visual interfaces. The scale of new public buildings is strictly controlled and folding roofs are used to continue the texture feature of the village and reduce the impact on the surrounding rural environment. At the same time, through the corridors, ramps, and landscape platform systems of different elevations, the scattered buildings are closely connected to form a public "rural complex" with efficient functions and pleasant spaces. From the design to the construction process, our team went through multiple deliberations on the selection of materials and finally selected common local masonry, bamboo, and wood combined with lightweight steel and aluminum profiles to achieve a balance between local characteristics and spatial economic performance. In addition, several multi-scale mockups were deliberated on some key details, and 1:1 trials and inspections were carried out at the sites to ensure the final quality of completion.

In the design of Qinglong Square, Oil Mill Museum Square, and the courtyard of rural ecological restaurant, the historical remains of original industrial facilities in the sites such as the Qinglong Sculpture, old factory buildings, and biogas tank were carefully assessed. Then, according to their quality conditions and functional spatial needs, different modes of conservation and renovation such as appearance restoration, structural replacement, element cutting, and offsite reconstruction were adopted to make a good combination of old and new buildings into the overall spatial creation of the building groups, reshaping the texture feature of the village while continuing the collective memory of the local residents.

From conception, design to final completion, we have experienced a lot in this project. This practice is facing an integrated design and construction project from village and industrial planning, architectural and landscape design to interior decoration and exhibition arrangement. Although our team is not responsible for all these design works, we must have a comprehensive study of the whole cycle in order to achieve a good expression of rural history and culture with local characteristics at different scales. At the same time, rural architectural practice is often faced with more diverse user groups and functional needs, especially in villages with a high proportion of indigenous like Donglong. It is important to carefully consider the different demands of foreign visitors and local residents, which can reduce the designer's single "aesthetic value output". In addition, more communication with village collective to form a good and mutual assistance "community of rural construction" can compensate for the separation from the real life of the village due to market-oriented and standardized construction to a certain extent. In fact, we have observed that after the completion of these groups of buildings, some residents have used them as a reference to renovate their homes or shops in various ways according to their needs, which shows that this rural construction work has played a good role as a model.

The completion and operation of the building renovation of Donglong Village have received widespread attention and gained some positive comments. The villagers have held more and more various special activities in these new squares, and the rural industrial service business has been more fully expanded. At the same time, many party-building works have been carried out in an orderly manner relying on the village hall. But we are also soberly aware that the building renovation in Donglong Village is still worthy of further improvement and enhancement in terms of material weathering research, control of construction progress, and construction accuracy, so we look forward to learning from our experience and reducing regrets in our future rural practice.

Finally, thanks must be given to all those who made important contributions to the planning, design, and construction of Donglong Characteristic Rural Areas project, including Jiangning District People's Government, Jiangning Branch of Nanjing Municipal Bureau of Planning and Natural Resources, Qinglong Community, and Huachengboyuan Engineering Technology Group Co., Ltd., etc.

2023. 06

目录　CONTENTS

01	背景	Background	17
02	规划	Planning	25
03	建筑	Architecture	39
04	后续	Follow-up	103

01 背景
Background

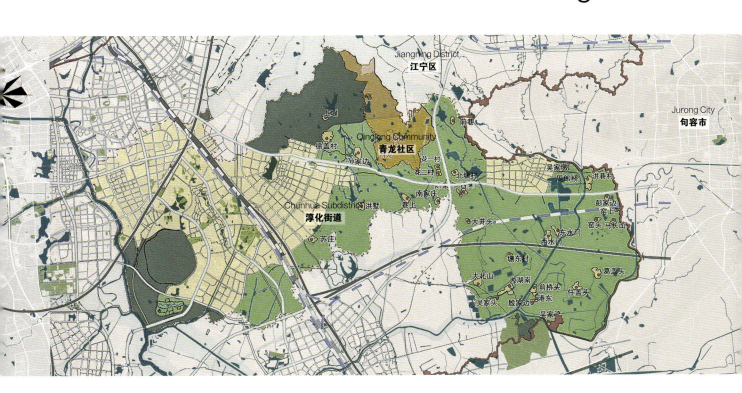

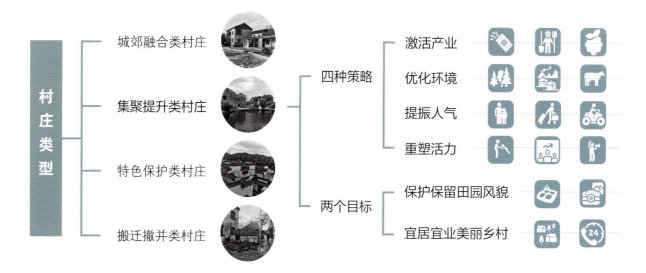

国家"乡村振兴战略"
National Rural Vitalization Strategy

2017 年 10 月 18 日,习近平同志在党的十九大报告中提出要实施乡村振兴战略。十九大报告指出,农业农村农民问题是关系国计民生的根本性问题,必须始终把解决好"三农"问题作为全党工作重中之重。要坚持农业农村优先发展,按照产业兴旺、生态宜居、乡风文明、治理有效、生活富裕的总要求,建立健全城乡融合发展体制机制和政策体系,加快推进农业农村现代化。

2018 年 1 月 2 日,国务院公布了 2018 年中央一号文件,即《中共中央国务院关于实施乡村振兴战略的意见》,明确了分阶段实现乡村振兴战略的目标任务。2018 年 9 月,中共中央、国务院印发《乡村振兴战略规划(2018—2022年)》(以下简称《规划》)。自此,乡村振兴战略的内涵更为全面丰富。《规划》对实施乡村振兴战略做出阶段性谋划,并通过细化实化工作重点和政策措施,部署重大工程、重大计划、重大行动,确保战略的落实落地。

《规划》明确提出了"分类推进乡村发展"的策略,即:顺应村庄发展规律和演变趋势,根据不同村庄的发展现状、区位条件、资源禀赋等,按照集聚提升、融入城镇、特色保护、搬迁撤并的思路,分类推进乡村振兴,不搞一刀切。

On October 18, 2017, President Xi Jinping proposed to implement the strategy of rural vitalization in the report of the 19th CPC National Congress. The report pointed out that issues relating to agriculture, rural areas and rural people are fundamental to China as they directly concern our country's stability and our people's wellbeing. Addressing these issues should have a central place on the work agenda of the Party and we must prioritize the development of agriculture and rural areas. To build rural areas with thriving businesses, pleasant living environments, social etiquette and civility, effective governance, and prosperity, we need to put in place sound systems, mechanisms, and policies for promoting integrated urban-rural development, and speed up the modernization of agriculture and rural areas.

On January 2, 2018, the State Council announced the No. 1 Central Document of 2018, which clarified the strategic objectives and tasks of rural vitalization to be achieved in stages. In September, 2018, the National Rural Vitalization Strategic Plan (2018-2022) (hereinafter referred to as the Plan) was issued. Since then, the connotation of the rural vitalization strategy has become more comprehensive and rich. The Plan makes a phased plan for the implementation of the rural vitalization strategy, and through detailed and actual work priorities and policy measures, plans and action are deployed to ensure the implementation of the strategy.

The Plan clearly proposed the vitalization strategy of "promoting rural development by classification", that is, following the law of village development and evolution trend, according to the development status quo, location conditions and resource endowments of different villages, according to the ideas of agglomeration and promotion, integration into cities and towns, characteristic protection, relocation and withdrawl, and promoting rural revitalization by classification, rather than making a one-size-fits-all approach.

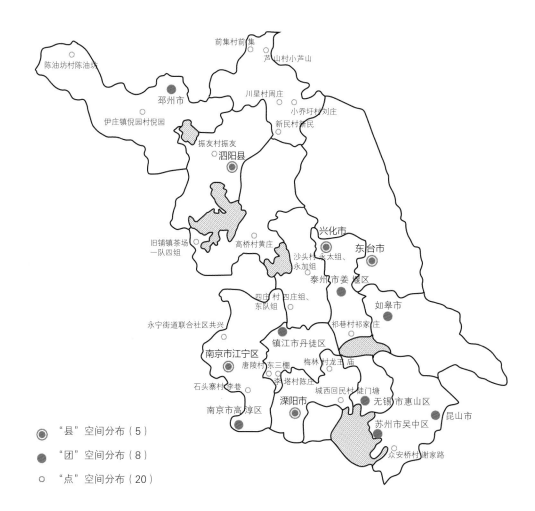

江苏省特色田园乡村
Characteristic Rural Areas in Jiangsu Province

2017 年 6 月，江苏省委、省政府正式印发《江苏省特色田园乡村建设行动计划》，以"生态优、村庄美、产业特、农民富、集体强、乡风好"为总体目标实现乡村振兴。相比于"美丽乡村"建设，特色田园乡村建设不仅重视村庄环境，也强调村庄周边田园、山水环境的保育和提升；不仅致力于乡村旅游业的发展，也重点关注乡村特色产业发展以及产业的综合；不仅注重对乡村历史文物的保护，也深入挖掘转译乡土文化、乡贤文化和乡村本土性特色。特色田园乡村建设不是"美丽乡村"建设的延续，而是具有更加宏观和统筹性的视野，以弥补早期乡村建设统筹不足带来的问题。

按照地方推荐、联合会商、地域统筹、涵盖多种农业产业类型、兼顾探索经济薄弱村脱贫等原则，首批省级特色田园乡村形成了"5 县 8 团 20 个点"试点候选地区和村庄名单。南京市江宁区入选首批试点村庄候选名单"5 县"之一，开展 5 个田园特色乡村建设试点，侧重于县域的工作推进和机制创新振兴。

In June 2017, the Jiangsu Provincial Party Committee and the Provincial Government formally issued the Provincial Characteristic Rural Areas Construction Action Plan, aiming to achieve the overall goal of "excellent ecology, beautiful villages, special industries, rich farmers, strong collectives, and good rural customs". The construction of characteristic rural areas not only pays attention to the village environment, but also emphasizes the preservation and improvement of the rural, landscape and environment surrounding the village. The action commits to the development of rural tourism as well as rural characteristic industries. Rural historical cultural relics are protected by digging into the translation of rural culture, rural sage culture and rural local characteristics. With a more macroscopic and overall perspective, the action aims to make up for the problems caused by the lack of overall planning for early rural construction.

In accordance with several principles, the first batch of provincial level characteristic rural villages formed the pilot candidate areas and villages of "5 counties, 8 groups and 20 spots" List. Jiangning District of Nanjing was selected as one of the "5 counties", and launched 5 rural village construction pilots, focusing on county work promotion and mechanism innovation and revitalization.

江宁区从"美丽乡村"到"特色田园乡村"
From "Beautiful Village" to "Characteristic Rural Areas" in Jiangning District

"美丽乡村"一词在乡村建设中广泛运用,其概念最初在党的十六大上第一次明确提出,后由 2013 年中央一号文件正式阐述,其具体内容主要包含"生产发展、生活宽裕、乡风文明、村容整洁、管理民主"等要求。在各省市的推进落实中,"美丽乡村"建设包含了一系列具体的建设工作。

南京市江宁区"美丽乡村"建设是中央政策落地实践的缩影,也是江宁从工业开发园区导向的发展模式向城乡互动、多产业统筹发展模式逐渐转化的过程,从 2011 年开始至今,一共经历了四个阶段的发展。

具体来看,"美丽乡村"建设的第一阶段由政府主导,集中打造"五朵金花"美丽示范村,通过农家乐开发、整治、优化乡村风貌和空间,吸引城市人群;第二阶段以政府带动多元投资,"以点带面"扩大示范区域;第三阶段建立多元主体长效合作机制,拟定多层次的建设导则,以"千村整治、百村示范"计划覆盖 70% 的村庄;第四阶段以品质发展、功能弥合、特色塑造为主要内容,以"特色田园乡村"推动乡村从基础建设到特色文化培育,从单一旅游向乡村复合产业发展。

The term "beautiful village" is widely used in rural renovation projects. Its content mainly includes "production development, rich life, civilized rural style, clean environment, democratic management" and other requirements. In the implementation of various provinces and cities, the construction of "beautiful village" includes a series of specific construction work.

The construction of "beautiful villages" in Jiangning District, Nanjing is the epitome of the central government's policy implementation. It is also the process of the gradual transformation from an industry-oriented development model to an urban-rural interaction and multi-industry coordinated development model. Since 2011, It has experienced four stages of development.

The first stage is led by the government, focusing on building "five golden flowers" as models, and optimizing the rural space through the development and renovation of farmhouses to attract urban people. The second stage focuses on driving multiple investment, expands the demonstration area by "points and areas". The third stage establishes a long-term cooperation mechanism with multiple subjects, and draws up multi-level construction guidelines. The fourth stage aims at qualified and featured development. The "characteristic rural area" is used to promote the development of rural areas from infrastructure construction to characteristic cultural cultivation, from single tourism to rural composite industries.

02 规划
Planning

南京市江宁区
Jiangning District, Nanjing

青龙社区
Qinglong Community

东龙—西龙村域
Donglong-Xilong Village Area

地理区位　　Location of Donglong Village

东龙村位于江苏省南京市的东南近郊，处于江宁区淳化街道青龙社区的现代农业示范区内。村域交通便利，又邻近S337省道、G104国道，距主城区约1小时车程。村庄毗邻西龙村，在北侧与青龙山遥遥相望，视野开阔，景观优美，地理区位条件较优越。

Donglong Village is located in the southeastern suburb of Nanjing, Jiangsu Province, and is within the modern agricultural demonstration park of Qinglong Community, Chunhua Subdistrict, Jiangning District. The village area is conveniently located near the S337 Provincial Road and the G104 National Road, about one hour's drive from the main urban area. The village is adjacent to Xilong Village, facing Qinglong Mountain on the north side, with broad view and beautiful landscape, and its geographical location is superior.

02 规划 Planning

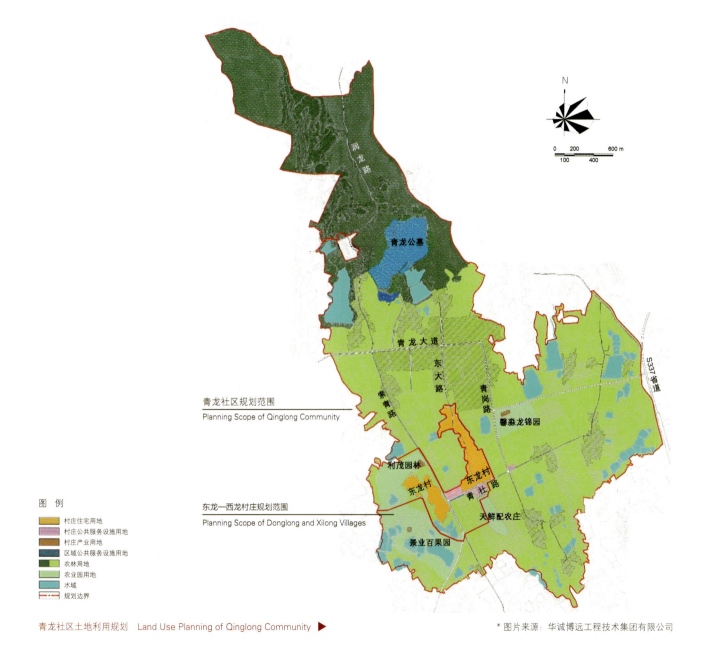

青龙社区土地利用规划　Land Use Planning of Qinglong Community ▶

村域规划　Planning of Donglong and Xilong Villages

东龙村和西龙村相互毗邻，位于青龙社区西南部，是社区保留的两个自然村。村域地形平坦，水资源丰富，土壤和气候条件适宜，农业基础较好。目前村庄周边已形成一定规模的苗木、瓜果、蔬菜、茶叶和中草药等的培育与种植区，同时龙王庙、清凉庵等众多历史人文遗迹也分布其中。近年来，随着田园体验旅游逐渐升温，村庄周边的南京鑫淼龙锦园、景业百果园等休闲旅游园区吸引了越来越多的城市观光人群，与之相关的电商服务产业也在不断拓展之中。2018年，东龙村入选江苏"特色田园乡村"试点，启动村庄建设工作。

依托现有的自然和人文资源，规划提出"守望相助新邻里，百果争鲜微电商"的总体发展目标，旨在通过对产业模式的调整优化和公共空间环境的整合提升，形成"一区四片"的空间格局，推动村域在生态、生产和生活三方面的全面发展。

在生态方面，规划严控村域建设用地范围，完善雨污工程的建设以保护水土环境健康，同时合理规划周边农业园区，打造有特色的田园景观和宜人的生态环境；在生产方面，依托现有农业资源，鼓励农业与电商的协同互助，拓展集合农业生产、农产品加工、休闲观光、生态康养、电商服务等的合作经济模式，以促进"一、二、三"产业的协同发展；在生活方面，进一步完善道路交通、综合防灾和社区公共服务设施的建设，同时打造重要空间节点，传承和发扬当地历史文化，建设有特色、有归属感的乡村生活环境。

双村联动发展
Collaborative Development

特色林果培育
Characteristic Fruit Cultivation

Donglong and Xilong villages are adjacent to each other and are the two natural villages preserved in Qinglong Community. The village area has a good agricultural foundation, and a certain scale of cultivation and planting area of seedlings, fruits, vegetables, tea and Chinese herbs has been formed around the village, while many historical and cultural relics such as Longwang Temple and Qingliang Nunnery are also distributed there. In recent years, with the gradual heating up of rural experience tourism, the leisure tourism gardens around the village have attracted more and more urban sightseeing people, and the related e-commerce service industry is also expanding. In 2018, Donglong Village was selected as one of the pilot projects of Jiangsu "characteristic rural areas" and started the construction of the village.

Relying on the existing natural and cultural resources, the planning puts forward the overall development goal of "a new neighborhood of mutual assistance with abundant and diversified agricultural e-commerce", aiming to form a spatial pattern of "one district with four pieces" by optimizing the industrial structure and improving the public environment, and promote the development of the village in three aspects: ecology, production and living conditions.

In terms of ecology, the planning controls the scope of construction land, and improves rainwater and sewage engineering to protect the soil and water environment. At the same time, agricultural gardens with distinctive rural landscape and ecological environment are reasonably planned in the surrounding area. In terms of production, the planning encourages synergy between agriculture and e-commerce, and expands the cooperative economic model that integrates agricultural production, processing, recreation, health care and e-commerce services, in order to promote the collaborative development of "primary, secondary and tertiary" industries. In terms of living, the construction of transportation, disaster prevention and public service facilities will be further improved, while important public space nodes will be designed to inherit and promote local culture and create a rural living environment with characteristics and a sense of belonging.

休闲农业服务
Leisure Agriculture Service

康养生态体验
Ecological Health Care Experience

▲ 村庄产业布局
Industry Distribution of the Village

东龙—西龙村域规划总平面图　Master Plan of the Donglong and Xilong Villages

*图片来源：华诚博远工程技术集团有限公司

东龙旧貌　Past of the Village

东龙村在空间形态上沿东大路呈南北带状分布,总体上呈现"田林环绕,星水伴居,悠然见山"的结构特征。村庄南侧的青社路为主要对外交通道路,目前道路两旁集中了主要的乡村公共服务设施,而在村庄中部和北侧相对缺乏。村庄建筑以两层民宅为主,部分单层老宅处于荒置状态。村内自然生态条件较好,分布了大小不一的水塘,大多以人工驳岸为主,主要水体水质较好;植被长势良好,现多分布于村民自家蔬菜和瓜果园或者宅基地周边的空地中。

目前在南侧道路交叉口和村庄中部,有几处村庄集体用地处于闲置状态,用地中包含青龙雕塑、老油坊、旧沼气站等建筑或构筑物历史遗存。基于现状环境条件和上位规划成果,团队选择了其中两个重点地块进行了详细调研。

Distributed in the north-south direction along Dongda Road, Donglong Village presents the characteristics of being "surrounded by fields and forests, accompanied with water ponds and mountains". The Qingshe Road on the south side of the village is the main external traffic road, and public service facilities are gathered on both sides of the road, while they are relatively lacking in the middle and north sides of the village. The village buildings were mainly two-story or three-story houses, and some of the old houses were in a deserted state. The natural ecological conditions in the village are excellent, with ponds of different sizes, and the water quality of its main water bodies is good, mostly with artificial revetments. The plants were growing well and mostly located in the villagers' own vegetable and fruit gardens or in the open spaces around their homesteads.

In the southern road intersection and middle of the village, there are several existing collective sites in an unused state, which contain historical remains of buildings such as the Qinglong Sculpture, the old oil mill and the old biogas station. Our team selected two important sites for a detailed survey.

更新前村庄总平面图　Past Master Plan of Donglong ▶

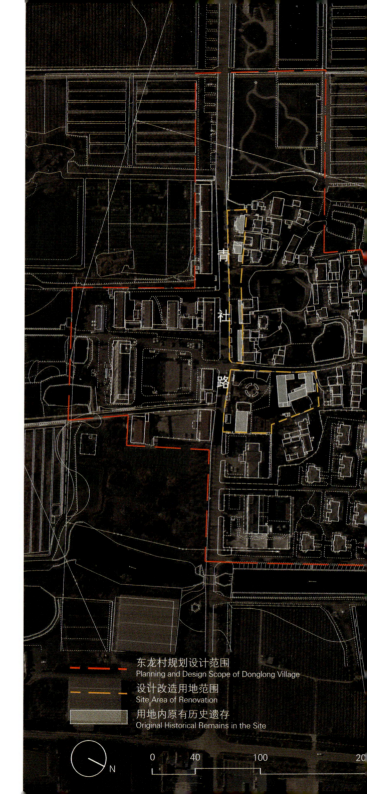

东龙村规划设计范围
Planning and Design Scope of Donglong Village

设计改造用地范围
Site Area of Renovation

用地内原有历史遗存
Original Historical Remains in the Site

02 规划 Planning

青社路
Qingshe Road

▲ 01 老油坊—电商街地块　Old Oil Mill and E-commerce Plot

▲ 02 旧沼气站地块　Original Biogas Station Plot

东龙新颜　　Present of the Village

设计团队充分研究东龙村自然和人文条件，结合城乡联动发展、农业－电商整合发展的宏观需求，对村庄空间结构和功能组织进行了统一的规划和设计。

首先，对选择的"老油坊－电商街地块"和"旧沼气站地块"两个重要空间节点进行详细的建设改造和更新设计，"以点带面"梳理村庄整体公共空间结构。通过场地原有历史遗存与新建筑的有机互动，在延续村民集体记忆的同时实现具有在地性特征的场所营造，以进一步吸引和带动多样化产业和人群的入驻，推动特色田园乡村的可持续发展。

其次，通过村庄整体环境设计提升公共景观品质，完善配套设施建设，满足新兴电商户、本地村民以及城市消费者日益提高的生活和空间需求。此外，对村庄中数量众多的民宅进行质量和风貌综合考察，针对老旧闲置住房、一般性住房和新建住房以导则形式分别提出差异化的改进策略和建议，鼓励村民和产业经营者在民宅建设中的自主发挥，实现村庄整体风貌的和谐与差异性并举。

Based on a full study of natural and cultural conditions, we plan and design an overall spatial and functional structure of Donglong Village considering the current needs of urban-rural coordinated development and the integration of e-commerce industries.

First of all, the two important sites of "old oil mill and e-commerce plot" and "original biogas station plot" were selected for detailed architectural renovation and renewal design. Through the interaction between the original historical relics and the new buildings, the collective memory of the villagers will be perpetuated and a place with local characteristics can be created, which will further attract and drive diversified industries and people to move in and promote the sustainable development of the characteristic rural areas.

Secondly, the quality of public landscape is upgraded through the overall environmental design of the village, which can improve the public facilities to satisfy the increasing spatial and functional needs of e-commerce merchants, local villagers and urban consumers. In addition, a comprehensive examination of the quality and style of the numerous residential houses in the village is conducted. Differentiated improvement suggestions are proposed in the form of guidelines for old and unused houses, general houses and new houses respectively, to encourage villagers to carry out independent construction of houses, achieving harmony and difference in the overall style of the village.

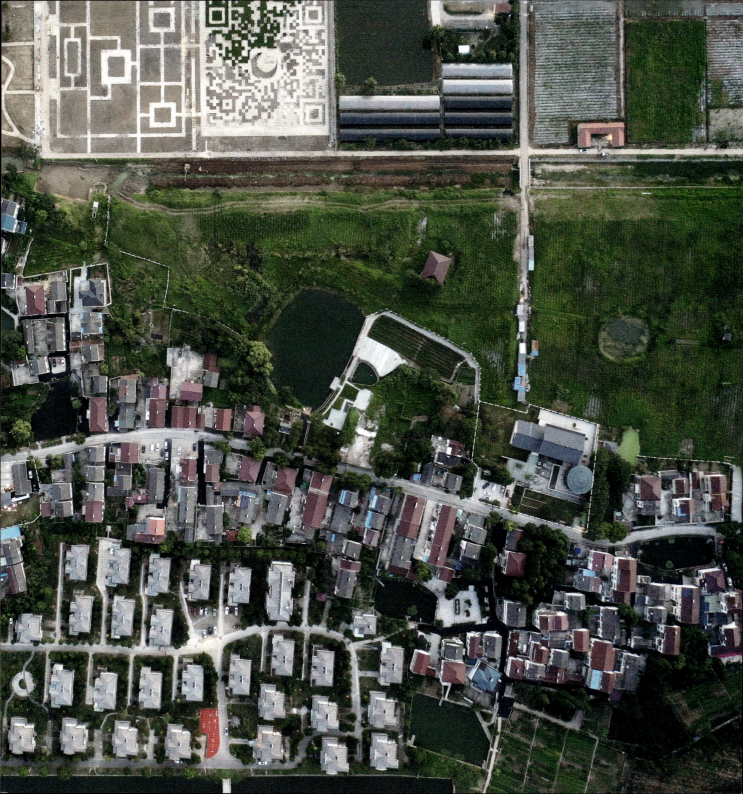

03 建筑
Architecture

03 建筑 Architecture

▼ 老油坊与青龙广场旧貌　Past of Old Oil Mill and Qinglong Square

1 老油坊 – 电商街地块
Old Oil Mill and E-commerce Plot

占地面积：约 6610 m²
Floor Area: about 6610 m²

建筑面积：约 3098 m²
Building Area: about 3098 m²

完成时间：2020
Completion Year: 2020

老油坊 – 电商街地块位于村口，内部原有青龙广场、老油坊、村民浴室、卫生站等闲置历史遗存。设计通过小体量分散布局和微介入改造的方式，在不破坏村庄风貌的基础上形成尺度适宜的村口公共建筑群，打造产业引导和存量资源整合并举的"乡村综合体"。

设计一方面统筹组合现有分散的乡村公共设施，并置入游客中心、村史馆、乡村会堂等新的功能，一同构成多组错落有致的院落空间；另一方面保留了原有广场的青龙雕塑和老油坊的部分厂房和设备遗存，改造更新为环绕开放庭院的"老油坊博物馆"，延续场所集体记忆。通过一系列结构置换和空间优化设计，使保留建筑与新功能空间、青龙广场形成宜人的乡村公共场所。

建筑形态上采用折屋顶延续村庄肌理，同时，新旧建筑群之间通过丰富的连廊、檐下敞厅、露台等空间连接，形成一系列公共活动和观景空间，满足不同年龄段的游客和当地村民在不同季节、不同时段的复合使用。

Old oil mill and e-commerce plot is located at the entrance of the village, with Qinglong Square, old oil mill, public bathhouse, health station, and and other unused historical remains inside. By means of a small-volume decentralised layout and micro-intervention renewal, the entrance of the village is transformed into a "rural complex" integrating industry guide and stock resources without destroying the texture features of the village.

On the one hand, the scattered rural public facilities are integrated and combined, and new functions such as Visitor Center, Village History Museum and Lecture Hall are implanted to form multiple groups of courtyard space; on the other hand, aiming to continue the memory of the place, the original Qinglong Sculpture and old production workshops are carefully preserved and have become a pleasant public space called "Old Oil Mill Museum" by structural replacement and space optimisation.

Folding roofs are used to continue the texture feature of the village, creating a series of public activities and viewing spaces between the new and old buildings through corridors, terraces, and open halls under eaves, which meets the compound use of tourists of different ages and local villagers in different seasons and at different time.

▼ 航拍图　Aerial Photograph

▲ 总平面　Master Plan

0 2 5 10m

1	青龙广场	Qinglong Square
2	青龙雕塑	Qinglong Sculpture
3	游客中心	Visitor Information Center
4	村史馆	Village History Museum
5	乡村会堂	Village Hall
6	乡村服务中心	Rural Service Center
7	油坊博物馆	Oil Mill Museum
8	乡村活动室	Rural Activity Room
9	老油坊遗址	Remains of Old Oil Mill
10	古木庭院	Tree Courtyard
11	游憩廊道	Recreation Corridor
12	油坊博物馆广场	Oil Mill Museum Square

西北侧航拍图　Aerial Photograph of the Northwest Side ▶

▲ 青龙广场透视　Perspective from Qinglong Square

03 建筑 Architecture

青龙广场局部　Part of Qinglong Square

◀ ▼ 边庭景观　View of Side court

03 建筑　Architecture

▲ 檐廊坡道　Ramp under Eaves

村民中心檐下空间　Perspective under Eaves

▲ 游憩平台　Recreation Platform

◀ 观景连廊　Viewing Corridor
▼ 转角台院　Corner Terrace Courtyard

▲ 东大路临街空间界面　Spatial Interface along Dongda Road

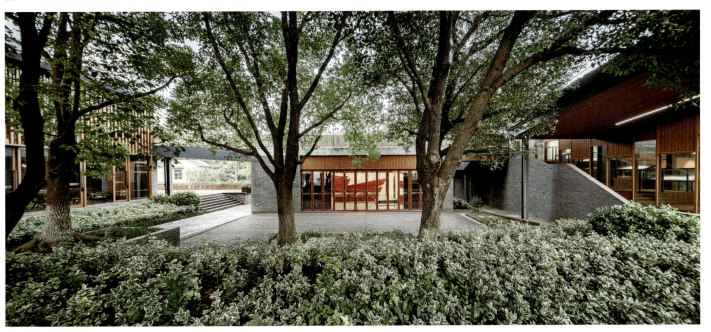

◀▲ 古木庭院　Tree Courtyard

庭院与广场景观局部　Part of Tree Courtyard and Square ▲

青龙雕塑与广场　Qinglong Sculpture and Square

▲ 油坊博物馆广场　Oil Mill Museum Square

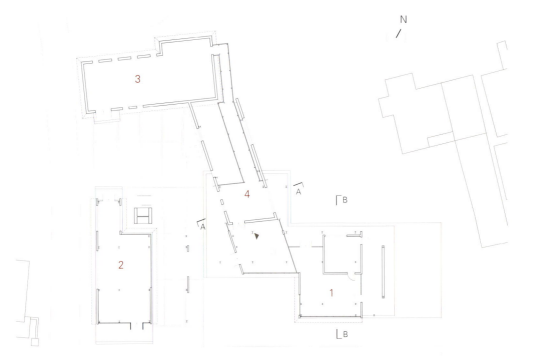

◀ 一层平面
First Floor Plan

1　乡村服务中心
　　Rural Service Center
2　乡村活动室
　　Rural Activity Room
3　油坊博物馆
　　Oil Mill Museum
4　展廊
　　Exhibition Gallery

03 建筑 Architecture

▲ 广场局部与油坊博物馆室内　Corner of Square and Interior View of Old Mill Museum

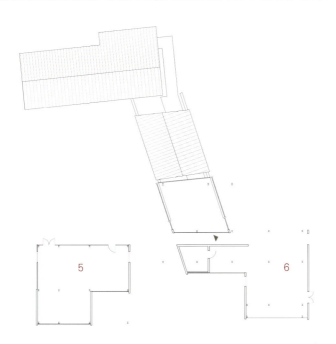

N

◀ 二层平面
　Second Floor Plan

5　乡村书屋
　Village Reading Room

6　茶餐厅
　Tea Restaurant

0　2　5　　10m

57

▲ 北侧油坊博物馆广场透视　Perspective from Oil Mill Museum Square (in the north)

03 建筑 Architecture

03 建筑 Architecture

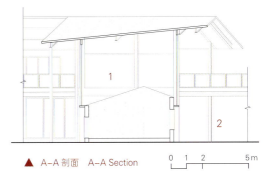

▲ A-A 剖面　A-A Section

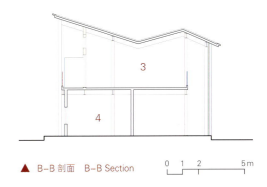

▲ B-B 剖面　B-B Section

1　展厅　Exhibition Hall
2　博物馆广场　Museum Square
3　茶餐厅　Tea Restaurant
4　乡村服务中心　Rural Service Center

◀ 东大路透视　Perspective from Dongda Road

▲ ▶ 博物馆展陈空间　Exhibition Space of Museum

03 建筑 Architecture

63

03 建筑 Architecture

◀ 村史馆展厅　Exhibition Halls in the Village History Museum

▲ 乡村议事厅 & 阅览空间　Village Council Room & Reading Room

▲ 室内展陈局部　Part of Interior Exhibition

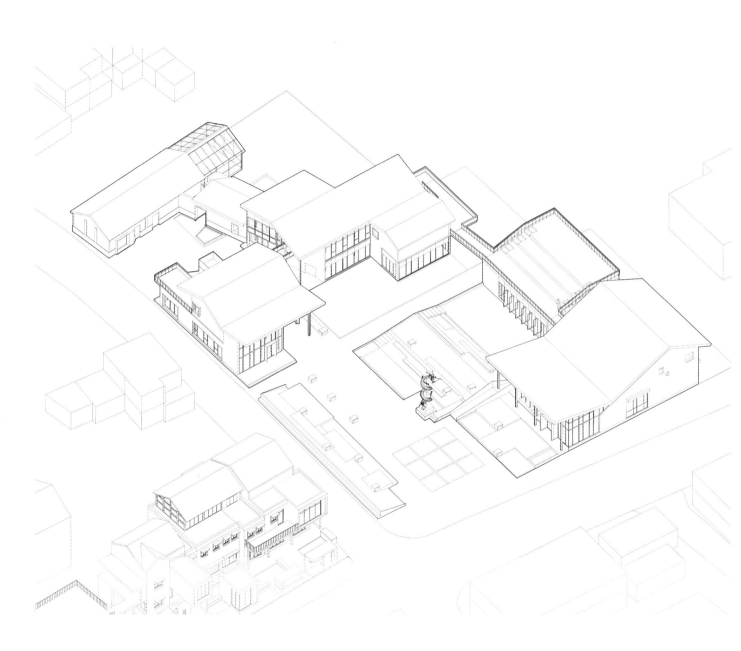

▲ 空间轴测　Space Axonometric

03 建筑 Architecture

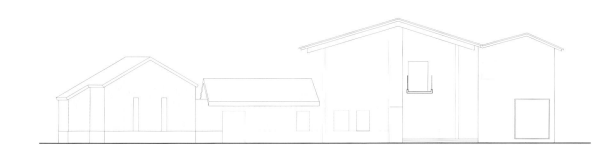

▲ 西立面图　West Elevation

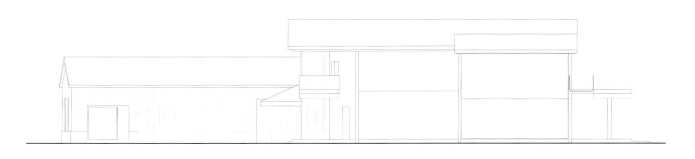

▲ 南立面图　South Elevation

▲ 轴测分解图　Exploded Axonometric Diagram

03 建筑 Architecture

▲ 乡村会堂室内　Interior View of Village Hall

▲ 村史展局部　Part of Village History Exhibition

▼ 青社路沿街夜景　Night View from Qingshe Road

▲ 边院夜景透视　Night View Perspective of Side Yard

▲ 古木庭院夜景透视　Night View Perspective of Tree Courtyard

03 建筑 Architecture

▼ 原沼气站旧貌　Past of Original Biogas Station

2 旧沼气站地块
Original Biogas Station Plot

占地面积：约 910 m²
Floor Area: about 910 m²

建筑面积：约 1375 m²
Building Area: about 1375 m²

完成时间：2020
Completion Year: 2020

旧沼气站地块位于村庄的中部，原有一栋闲置的厂房建筑和一个废弃的沼气罐。为平衡场地原有历史遗存与新功能空间需求，设计以"农产体验馆"为核心空间，整合周边各类田园，形成种植、大灶体验、果园采摘、生态农产品展销以及线上电商服务的联动发展。

首先，通过植入钢结构将原有厂房部分局部加高为二层，形成错落的屋面结构，满足复合功能使用的要求；然后，保留原有沼气罐并将其封闭的界面打开与院落产生空间互动，延续当地居民的集体记忆。同时，设计将建筑与道路之间的局部场地垫高为台地，以满足不同消费者以及当地居民多样化的活动需求。

在结构、立面和构造节点的推敲中，组合使用砖石和竹木等乡土材质配合轻质钢材、铝材等现代材质，建构出既具在地性又满足当代生活需求的空间特征。

The original biogas station plot, located in the middle of the village, contains a deserted industrial building and biogas tank. Considering the contradictory relationship between the relics of the site and new functions, a comprehensive "Agricultural Experience Exhibition Hall" is designed to integrate surrounding fields, forming a joint development of planting, cooking experience, fruit picking, ecological agricultural products exhibition and online e-commerce services.

Firstly, by implanting steel structures, the original factory building is partially raised to two floors, forming a staggered roof structure that meets the needs of composite functional use. Then, the original biogas tank is preserved and opened to create spatial interaction with the courtyard, continuing the collective memory of local residents. At the same time, the topography is partially elevated to form a terrace to meet the composite space requirements of different consumers and residents.

Local materials such as stone, bricks, bamboo and wood are used together with modern materials such as light steel and aluminum to construct local and contemporary space characteristics.

◀ 航拍图　Aerial Perspective

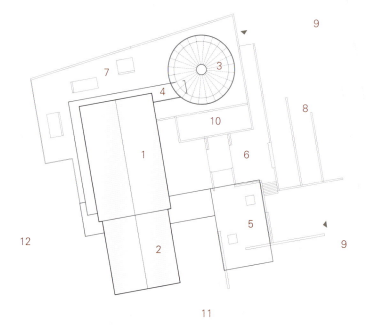

▲ 总平面 Master Plan

0 2 5 10m

1	农家"大灶"体验餐厅 Cooking Experience Hall		7	休憩边院 Side Yard
2	农产品展馆 Agricultural Product Pavilion		8	台地菜园 Terrace Vegetable Garden
3	户外展厅（原沼气罐） Original Biogas Tank		9	公共停车位 Public Parking
4	连廊 Connecting Corridor		10	池塘 Pond
5	公共休憩凉棚 Public Open Shelter		11	果园 Orchard
6	室外台院餐吧 Terrace Yard Dining Bar		12	特色药材种植区 Special Chinese Herb Planting Area

东南侧航拍图 Aerial Photograph of the Southeast Side ▶

▲ 西侧种植园透视　Perspective from Herb Plantation on the West Side

03 建筑 Architecture

▲ 东大路沿街透视（一） Perspective from Dongda Road (1)

03 建筑 Architecture

▲ 东大路沿街透视（二）　Perspective from Dongda Road (2)

室外台院餐吧　Terrace Yard Dining Bar ▲

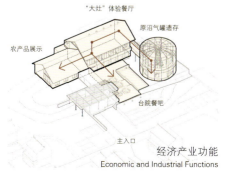

经济产业功能
Economic and Industrial Functions

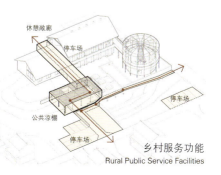

乡村服务功能
Rural Public Service Facilities

生态田园功能
Ecological and Pastoral Functions

◀ 东侧主入口　East Main Entrance

功能结构布局　Functional Structure ▲

▲ ▶ 公共休憩凉棚
Public Open Shelter

◀ 沼气罐新貌
Present of the Biogas Tank

西侧观景平台　Viewing Platform on the West Side ▶

▲ 台院餐吧局部　Part of Terrace Yard Dining Bar

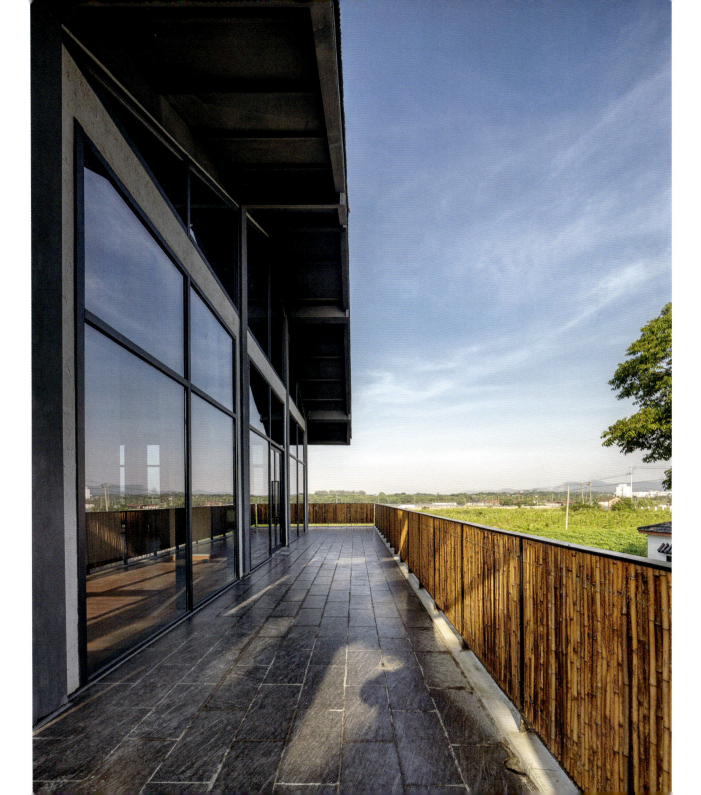

沼气罐新貌　Present of the Biogas Tank ▶

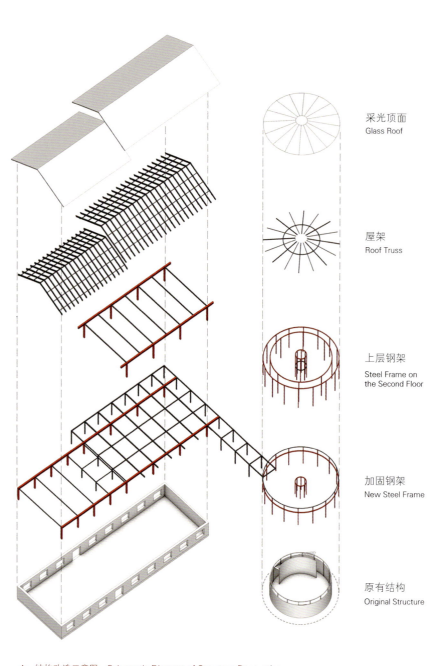

采光顶面
Glass Roof

屋架
Roof Truss

上层钢架
Steel Frame on the Second Floor

加固钢架
New Steel Frame

原有结构
Original Structure

▲ 结构改造示意图　Schematic Diagram of Structure Renovation

03 建筑 Architecture

▲ 屋架结构　Structure of Roof Truss

▲ 内部结构新貌　Present Structure of the Biogas Tank

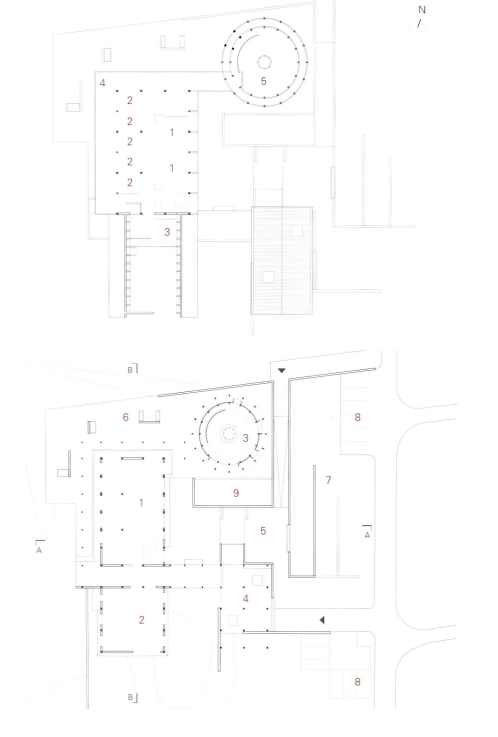

▸ 二层平面
Second Floor Plan

1 餐厅大包间
  Large Private Dining Room
2 餐厅卡座
  Dining Booth
3 洽谈休息间
  Lounge
4 观景平台 / 连廊
  Viewing Platform / Connecting Corridor
5 户外展厅（原沼气罐）上空
  Over the Original Biogas Tank

0 2 5 10 m

▸ 一层平面
First Floor Plan

1 农家"大灶"体验餐厅
  Cooking Experience Hall
2 农产品展馆
  Agricultural Product Pavilion
3 户外展厅（原沼气罐）
  Original Biogas Tank
4 公共休憩凉棚
  Public Open Shelter
5 室外台院餐吧
  Terrace Yard Dining Bar
6 休憩边院
  Side Yard
7 台地菜园
  Terrace Vegetable Garden
8 公共停车位
  Public Parking
9 池塘
  Pond

0 2 5 10 m

▲ 东侧主入口
East Main Entrance

▶ 水院局部
Part of Water Courtyard

▲ 室外台院餐吧　Terrace Yard Dining Bar

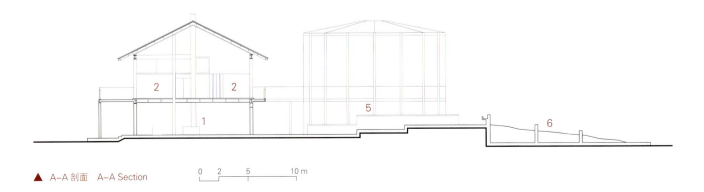

▲ A-A 剖面　A-A Section

03 建筑 Architecture

▲ 东立面与台院局部　East Facade and Part of Terrace Yard

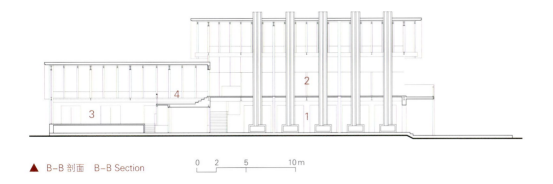

▲ B-B 剖面　B-B Section　　0　2　5　10 m

1　农家"大灶"体验厅
　　Cooking Experience Hall
2　餐厅
　　Dining Room
3　农产品展馆
　　Agricultural Product Pavilion
4　休息间
　　Lounge
5　室外台院餐吧
　　Terrace Yard Dining Bar
6　台地菜园
　　Terrace Vegetable Garden

95

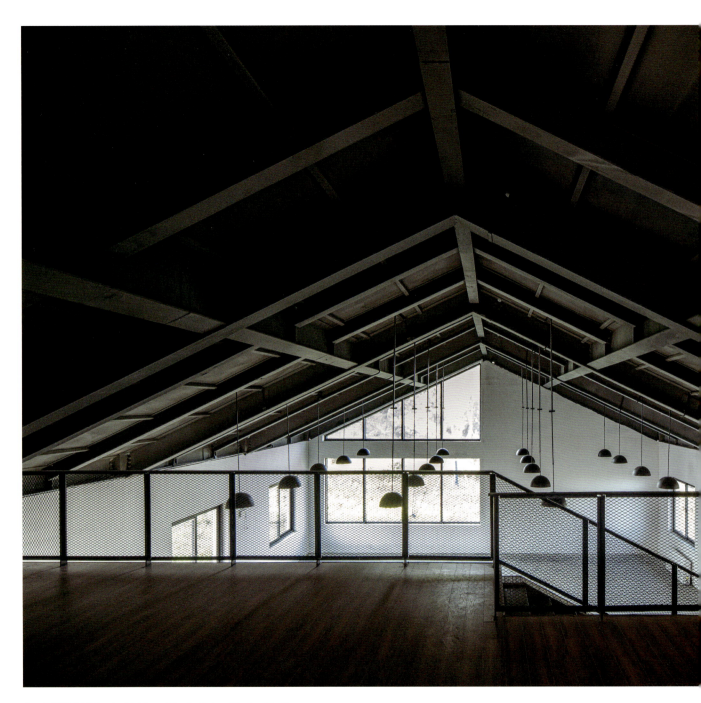

▲ 农产品展馆室内　Inside View of the Agricultural Product Pavilion

03 建筑 Architecture

▲ 二层室内　Inside View of the Second Floor

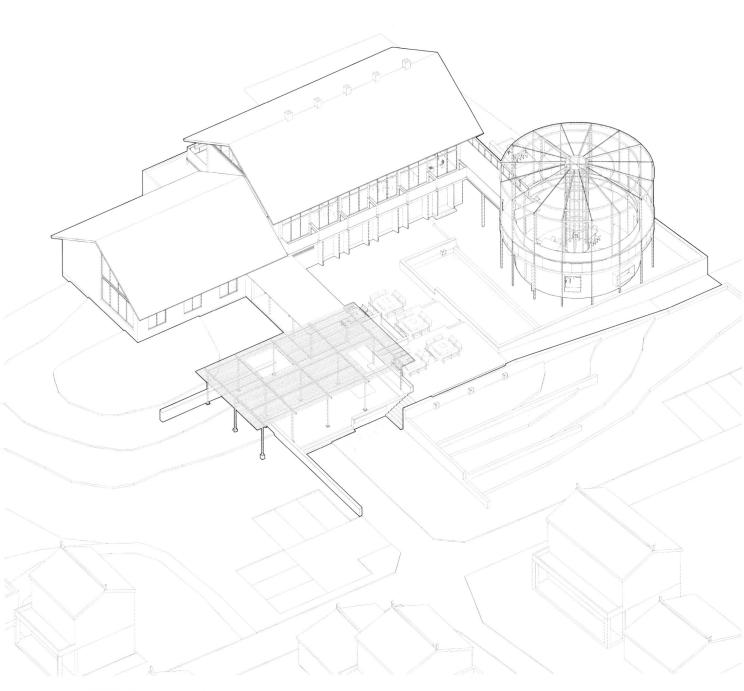

▲ 空间轴测　Space Axonometric

03 建筑 Architecture

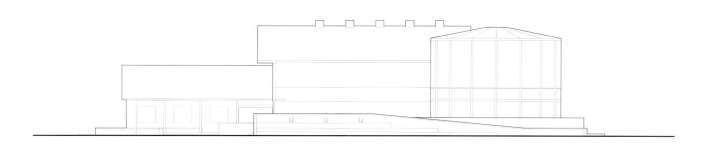

▲ 东立面图　East Elevation

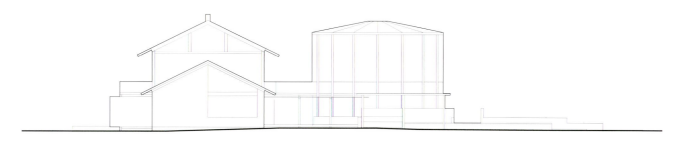

▲ 南立面图　South Elevation

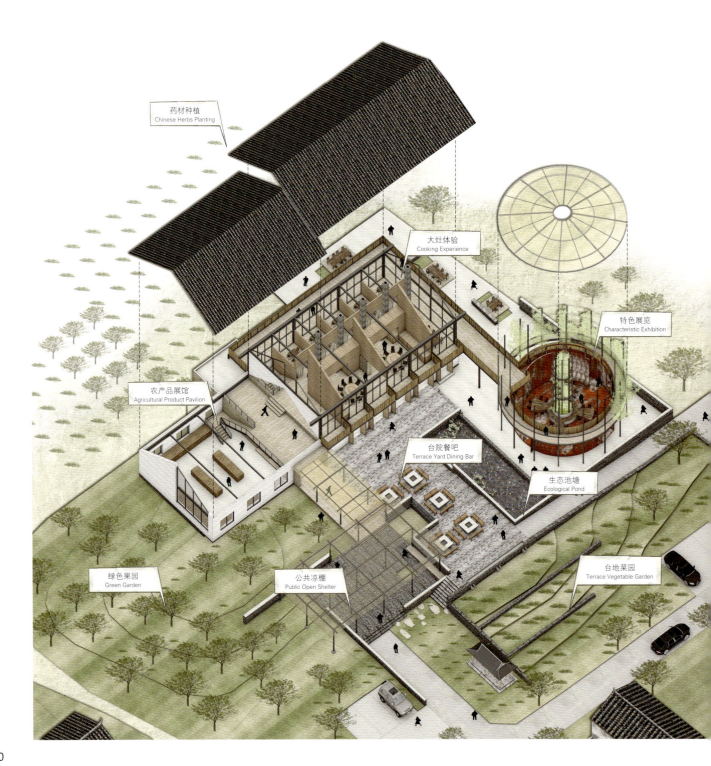

03 建筑 Architecture

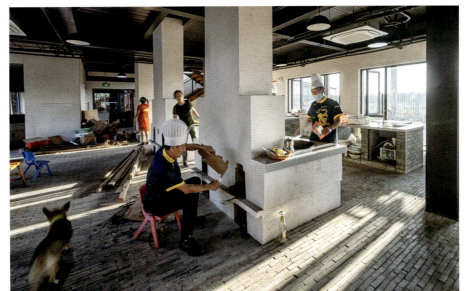

▲ "大灶"体验餐厅　Cooking Experience Hall

◀ 轴测分解图　Exploded Axonometric Diagram

04 后续
Follow-up

《青龙百姓的笑脸》 李延平 摄 ▲

宜活：打造乡居乐土
Activities of Rural Residents

在东龙村建设工作中，南京市规划和自然资源局江宁分局同街道和社区的特色田园乡村建设人员组成了专班小组，通过每周例会商讨相关建设计划，并不定期地现场解决施工问题，共同保证了村庄的建设品质。

经过本轮建设，东龙村公共服务设施容量得到较大提升，整体环境得到了综合整治，为居民生活和特色产业的持续发展提供了有力支撑。随着公共建筑群的竣工和运营，各类乡村党建工作、集体文娱和节庆活动得以更有序展开，丰富了村民的物质和精神生活，提升了村民的满足感和获得感，形成了宜居宜活的东龙乡居乐土。

在创建"特色田园乡村"后，东龙村在产业发展、生态环境、村庄治理等方面持续努力。2022年，村庄开始编制多规合一的实用性村庄规划，结合基本农田、生态红线的划定，进一步盘整村庄存量建设用地，为未来发展腾出更多空间。

In the rural construction of Donglong Village, Jiangning Branch of Nanjing Municipal Bureau of Planning and Natural Resources formed a task force team with Chunhua Subdistrict and Qinglong Community to discuss relevant construction plans through regular weekly meetings and to solve construction problems on site from time to time, together ensuring the construction quality of the village.

After this phase of construction, the capacity of public service facilities in Donglong Village has been greatly enhanced, and the overall environment has been comprehensively improved, providing strong support for the sustainable development of residents' lives and specialty industries. With the completion and operation of the public buildings, various types of village party building works, collective recreational and festive activities can be carried out in a more orderly manner, enriching the material and spiritual life of the villagers, enhancing their sense of satisfaction and gain, and forming a pleasant and livable Donglong countryside.

After the construction of "Characteristic Rural Areas", Donglong Village has continued its efforts in industrial development, ecological environment, and village governance. In 2022, combined with the delineation of basic farmland and ecological red lines, a practical multi-planning united for the village began to be prepared to further organize the construction land in the village, freeing up space for future development.

04 后续 / Follow-up

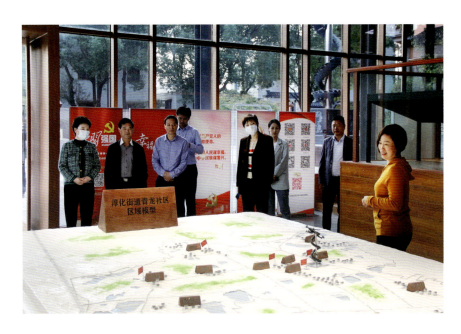

宜业：壮大农村集体经济
Rural Collective Economy with E-commerce

东龙村依托较好的农业环境和人口条件，逐渐发展起特色种植业和电商聚集区。在此基础上，社区成立了股份经济合作社，实现统一筹资、管理和用工，同时组织农技培训，引导村民就业创业，并通过集体经济发展的分红和困难群体补助造福百姓，实现利益共享，有效提高了村民的收入。

电商街建成后，乡村电商业务得以更有效拓展，进一步实现资源整合，探索农村集体经济多元化发展路径。一是特色种植业的规模扩大和质量提升，形成了千亩茶、瓜果、蔬菜和旅游农业观光区，荣获"省现代化农业示范区"；二是利用特色资源盘活集体资产，目前已形成多家企业和多种特色产品；三是依托服务设施深化乡村旅游，打造集合田园体验、科普教育和康养度假的综合项目，为城市游客带来具有地域特色和文化内涵的游览体验，实现城乡之间多产业的联动发展。

Relying on its good environment and population conditions, Donlong Village has gradually developed a characteristic plantation industry and an e-commerce gathering area. On this basis, the community set up a shareholding economic cooperative to achieve unified asset management and employment. At the same time, agricultural technology training was organized to guide villagers in employment, and the residents can benefit from dividends from collective economic development and subsidies for disadvantaged groups, effectively raising villagers' incomes.

After the completion of the e-commerce street, a variety of rural e-commerce businesses can be carried out more effectively to further integrate resources and explore the path of diversified development of the rural collective economy. Firstly, the scale and quality of the original characteristic planting industry have been expanded and improved, forming a vast area of tea, fruits and vegetables, and agricultural tourism garden, which won the title of "modern agricultural demonstration area in Jiangsu". Secondly, the collective assets of the village have been revitalized and a number of companies and characteristic products have been formed. Thirdly, the community has enhanced the quality of rural tourism relying on service facilities and created projects that integrate field experience, youth science education, and recreation degrees, providing urban visitors with a touring experience featuring local characteristics, and cultural connotations, and realizing the development of industrial linkages between urban and rural areas.

04 后续 / Follow-up

宜居：提升街道与社区服务
Service of Subdistrict and Community Office

在特色田园乡村建设中，淳化街道和青龙社区高度重视各方面的建议，组织多次考察学习活动，深入了解和解决各个阶段的问题和挑战，同时领导小组加大了人才引进和培养，高效统筹和推进各项工作。

乡村建设队伍在规划设计、建设以及运营的各个时期，充分征求当地村民的意见，实地走访和调研真实的建设情况，提升工作透明度。社区多次联合设计、施工团队进行方案优化，使空间设计、功能布局和材料选用上更加契合使用者的核心诉求，并合理安排施工计划以减少建设带来的生活干扰。在后期运营阶段，定期组织召开多方参与的协商议事会，了解广大居民后续建设愿景，增强民众对美丽宜居乡村建设的满意度和信任度。

同时，在建设过程中社区始终重视村集体中困难家庭、孤寡老人的生活，持续开展一系列主题活动、一对一帮扶、定期入户慰问和免费医疗等公共服务。

In the construction of the characteristic rural village, Chunhua Subdistrict and Qinglong Community attached great importance to the suggestions from various groups and organized many study tours to gain a deeper understanding and solve the problems and challenges. At the same time, the rural construction leading group has increased the introduction and training of talents to efficiently coordinate and promote all the works at various stages.

The rural construction team fully consulted villagers during all periods of planning, design, construction and operation, and visited and researched the real construction conditions to enhance the transparency of their work. The community has joined hands with the design and construction teams to optimize the functional layout and choice of materials to better suit the core requirements of the users, and to rationalize the construction schedule to reduce the disruption to life caused by construction. During the later operation phase, regular consultation meetings involving various groups were held to learn the general residents' vision for the subsequent construction, which can enhance their satisfaction and trust in the construction of a more beautiful and livable village.

At the same time, during the construction process the community has always attached importance to the living conditions and welfare of the needy families, elderly people who live alone in the village, and has continued to carry out a series of thematic activities, one-to-one support, regular visits and free medical care to households, and other public services.

建筑设计团队
Architectural Design Team

东龙村建筑改造更新在符合前期规划要求的基础上，严格按照设计方案实施，由东南大学建筑学院王建国院士团队进行重点建筑的更新设计。

设计团队对东龙各项目的选址、生态自然条件、场地历史遗存、建筑规模容量、产业功能类型等多方面予以了高度重视和充分研究，并对村庄整体规划、风貌控制和景观体系建设提出了系列建议。在村庄建设期间，设计团队多次到现场与当地社区、村民以及施工建设团队进行了充分沟通，不断优化设计和实施方案。

The building renovation of Donglong Village was implemented in strict accordance with the preliminary planning. The team of Academician Wang Jianguo from the School of Architecture of Southeast University attached great importance to this project.

The design team paid full attention to the site selection, ecological and natural conditions, historical relics, scale and capacity of the buildings, industrial function types and other aspects, and had put forward a series of suggestions on the overall village planning. During the construction period, our team visited the site several times to communicate with the local authorities, villagers and the construction team in order to optimize the design and implementation plan.

04 后续 / Follow-up

项目负责人	王建国　朱　渊
规划管理部门	南京市规划和自然资源局江宁分局
参与方案设计人员	东南大学建筑学院
原油坊地块改造设计	乔炯辰　常　胤
电商街改造更新	张皓翔　奚月林
旧沼气站改造设计	罗文博　沈宇驰
施工图设计单位	正中国际项目管理集团有限公司
建筑施工图设计	范　诚　刘文军　章平平　周顺云
结构设计	师厚飞　高　翔
给排水设计	吕　静
电气设计	王学峰
暖通设计	冯纪平
景观设计	陈天娇　郭玲娜
展陈策划人员	
设计与统筹	毛聿川
空间设计	张　敏　孙　程
视觉设计	金　涛
展陈工艺	沈　立
前期规划设计	华诚博远工程技术集团有限公司
摄影	王建国院士团队　许昊皓　青龙社区等
本书编撰人员	罗文博　宗袁月